The AMERICAN WITCHES

Coloring Book

50 POWERFUL WOMEN IN BLACK AND WHITE

SALLY ECKHOFF

Designer Credits
Cover Art by Sally Eckhoff
Interior by Anna Zubrytska
Author Photo by Dona Ann McAdams

Library of Congress Cataloging-in-Publication Data is available.
ISBN: 978-1-62134-450-6

To all the women trying to get their potions made.

ACKNOWLEDGMENTS

To the women who were pushed to prominence by the loss of people
they love, through your sorrow I hope you can see
how grateful we are.

AUTHOR'S NOTE:

"I never declared myself a witch. I just remembered I was one."

~ anonymous Facebook posting ~

What's a witch? Look for her silhouette—a woman in an old-fashioned black bombazine dress with a pointy hat and a pointy chin and a pointy nose that reaches around toward the tip of her chin. She's not undead; she's curiously eternal. And yet a witch is a real person—just not one that everybody is brave enough to meet. Witches are reviled, feared, attacked. But witches are admired, too, and in this book we give them all the love they've been missing. Every day, a new witch appears in the nighttime sky. Why? Because we need her. With witch applications up, the approval process is as gnarly as ever. So we need a way let the witches show their stuff.

Why witches? There are times and places where only something catalytic will get the job done. Witches have that special ability to make ordinary things—brooms, for instance—do extraordinary things, in order to get to an ultimate objective, which is to *mess someone up*. There's nothing you can do to stop a witch, and when you get onto her list, you're gonna feel it.

How did witches get so big in contemporary culture? It took a while. All those love songs, the ones that go, "She broke my heart," were just the latest fan to their flame. "She broke my heart, ergo she's a witch," finally found its own reaction. If that's the way they want it, then we're all witches. The line forms right here.

To give American Witches their proper due, we found criteria that emphasize new forces in our society. An American Witch is, for our purposes, someone who's alive right now. She has to be able to catalyze her resources into powers—a talent that can surprise even the witch herself. Lastly, she has to be willing to use those powers, and damn the consequences. She can't be in it for the money.

New witches are swooping over our horizons every day. Who did we miss? Send us your Witch suggestions at https://mailchi.mp/waterstreetpressbooks/american-witches.

Fifty percent of the profits from this coloring book will be donated to Stacey Abrams's voting rights organization, Fair Fight (https://fairfight.com) because witches, well, we have each other's backs.

And because voting is the most important thing a person can do, witch or not.

Now find your broom and get ready to ride.

Kamala Harris

"I'm speaking!," the woman said, and now everybody knows it means SHUT UP or else. You think you get to be the first female Vice President (of color, South Asian) by letting measly pretenders like Mike Pence talk over you? Kamala Harris spanked Joe Biden during the debates, she made Brett Kavanaugh cry, and she's gonna be president some day. Mamala, Kamala, you could set the world on fire, but please, just be our witch; get up there and *burn*.

Beyonce

It could be the gorgeous and expensive production, the closeness of her voice to the surface of the music, or her willingness to disappear in the middle of a chord: Beyonce is a kind of extra-human singer. She does a thing with her eyes when she's dancing in Formation that says, "You with me?", inviting complicity and more of that good trouble. Remember, "You can't wear a crown wit'cha head down."

Tammy Duckworth

An Army helicopter pilot grievously injured in the Iraq war, she was elected to the House of Representatives in 2012, and has served as the junior U.S. Senator from Illinois since 2017. Tammy Duckworth is the first Thai American woman elected to Congress, the first woman with a disability elected to congress, the first female double amputee in the Senate, the first senator to have a baby while in office, and the last military vet you'd want to insult if you were a five-time draft deferment president. That's how Trump got to be Cadet Bone Spurs.

Melissa McCarthy

Shape-shifting comic actress who specializes in playing nefarious men on SNL, McCarthy is as close to a drag king as anyone on TV. Only it's the idea of hiding her femininity that makes the joke. She can do Sean Spicer driving a podium down 5th Avenue in New York, or Rudy Giuliani, who's so bizarre to begin with—but she's always herself, the slyest identity trick of all.

Nancy Pelosi

Only recently does she have any competition as a woman in Washington. She's been the most feared witch in Foggy Bottom ever since she became the first female Speaker of the House, and is arguably the most powerful woman in America right now. Why does the right hate her? How much time have you got? This feared witch will be flossing with Mitch McConnell's tendons before this is over.

Tina Fey

The queen of Obama-era political satire, she's the reason why Sarah Palin can't go out in public anywhere besides Alaska. Tina doesn't have enough shelves in her house for all the awards she's won, but the Mark Twain Prize for American Humor might be her favorite.

Rosalinda Lopez

This young RN became the face of the vaccination movement the day she took her first COVID injection and flexed for the camera. Her muscular energy and can-do smile was so close to the iconic 1943 "We Can Do It" poster, she's proved that the new Rosie the Riveter is a health care worker. Thanks, Rosalinda!

Patti Smith

Should we call her Aunt Patti, or Saint Patti? The never-say-die icon of '70s punk stuck around long enough to recreate herself as a traveling sage. Being a symbol for the entire New Wave movement interested her a lot less than chronicling her adventures with her photographer friend, Robert Mapplethorpe—thus ensuring a lasting, museum-quality legacy.

Tamika Palmer

Ms. Palmer suffered the loss of her daughter, Breonna Taylor, at the hands of police in March 2020. And then she and her family won a $12 million wrongful death lawsuit against the Louisville, KY police department. "I'm not going away," she announced. "For me, every day is still March the 13th."

Jane Fonda

Anybody who believed F. Scott Fitzgerald when he said there are no second acts in American life has never seen Jane Fonda. She could be a cool Frenchified starlet, an intergalactic bombshell, or a rabble-rouser visiting Angela Davis in jail. Being Hanoi Jane the misguided peace protester almost eradicated her social currency. But she came back with movies: *Coming Home, The China Syndrome*, and especially *9 to 5*. Jane is 80+ and still getting arrested—five times in 2019 alone, for her Fire Drill Friday protests.

Stacey Abrams

By having a personal hand in turning Georgia blue during the 2020 elections, Stacey Abrams became a major player in national politics. She fought 45's efforts to limit voting in Georgia, and kept voting rights—our founding principle and the taproot of our democracy—in the foreground of the political landscape. The fight ain't over but I feel safer getting in formation behind Ms. Abrams.

Megan Rapinoe

This soccer champ is the most famous woman in sports after beating the Netherlands in the finals of the 2019 soccer World Cup. But word came around that you-know-who might like to meet her. Good luck with that. "I don't want to go to the fucking White House," she snarled. Rapinoe's girl-friend Sue Bird told *Vanity Fair* that Rapinoe is "the world's biggest most kissable goofball queen" and scored all those goals *because she's queer.*

RBG

The late Supreme Court justice Ruth Bader Ginsburg earned so many superlatives that we don't feel the need to add any more. But here: First woman to lie in state in the US capitol rotunda. First female Jewish justice. First in her class at Cornell, 1954. First in her class at Columbia Law School. Not the first female Supreme Court justice: that was Sandra Day O'Connor. She still established herself as a champion of women's rights who wanted a fair fight above all—and won.

Michelle Wolf

Who else has hair this wild and a voice this shrill and could bite your head off and still be hungry? Give Michelle Wolf five minutes and she'll dump so many witty apercus on your head you won't be able to stand up. Women want to be superior to men: "Admit it! You want to line the streets with tampons and fill the fountains with Chardonnay." What's standing in our way? Men, not because they make us uncomfortable, but because they make us comfortable: "It's hard to start a revolution from under a duvet."

Lisa Page

A former FBI lawyer and Federal prosecutor who cut her teeth on the Boston bombing and Edward Snowden's leaks in 2013, Lisa Page was a career public servant who wound up the target of a Trump smear campaign. The DOJ was reading the texts she sent to her married lover, an FBI agent named Peter Strzok. And along comes Rudy Giuliani to shovel on some hyperbole and maybe make her die from shame. Lisa Page shone a light onto how far the Trumpfolk would go to destroy anybody who just plain didn't like them. Once again, they were barking up the wrong witch.

Rachel Maddow

The thorn in the side of every conservative who's paying attention, Rhodes scholar Rachel Maddow took special care in observing the Trump organization's Russia-meddling misdeeds. Capable of biting sarcasm, Rachel is nevertheless more of a power nerd than a gadfly. That she manages to do her job without cursing a blue streak qualifies her as a Witch Transcendent.

Stacey Plaskett

There is this guy named Glenn Grothman, serving Wisconsin in the House of Representatives. And to his everlasting regret, there's also Congresswoman Stacey Plaskett, formerly an impeachment manager, representing the Virgin Islands. The House was debating the COVID rescue package when Grothman came out with this lulu: *Black Lives Matter doesn't like the old-fashioned family.* Plaskett reminded him pointedly that Black people have been able to keep their families alive during more than 400 years of an agenda for there not to be Black families or any Black lives at all. "How dare you say we are not interested in families in the Black community? That is outrageous. That should be stricken down." Loud applause.

Samantha Bee

This Canadian-American comic started out with Jon Stewart on *The Daily Show* and went on to host her own *Full Frontal* with an extra dollop of smiling crudeness. She's less reserved than Rachel M., who for all her erudition has never had the nerve to call the Former Guy "toilet clog".

LaShandra Rayfield

This school administrator and mother confronted some guys at Edison Beach in Illinois because they hung up a Confederate Flag towel—draped it over the fence as a kind of invitation for other bigots to hang out. They wouldn't take it down, so Rayfield videoed the confrontation, which consisted mostly of her explaining loudly why it wasn't cool. Then she put it on Facebook. The town's (white) mayor backed her up, there was a nice protest, and the flag jerks vamoosed. Small venue, major witch.

Mazie Hirono

She's the Senator from Hawaii who made Amy Comey Barrett get that deer-in-the-headlights look during her confirmation hearings, and worked in a scathing critique of the Trump administration's COVID response at the same time. Nice work from the Senate's only immigrant and also its first female Asian-American (she was elected to the Senate four years earlier than Tammy Duckworth). And that wasn't all, not nearly. Mazie's quiet, but her words pack a powerful punch. During the Kavanaugh hearings, she said what we'd all like to hear: "I just want to say to the men in this country: Just shut up and step up. Do the right thing, for a change."

Patti Lupone

This fierce Broadway singer—she played Evita Peron, remember?—has Grammys, Tonys, two Olivier awards, and a special way of talking. You can watch a video (over and over again) of her being buttonholed by a *Variety* reporter on the red carpet of the Tony awards. Should President Trump come see her new show?, he asked. No, she said; she wouldn't perform if he showed up. The writer asked why. "Because I hate the motherfucker. How's that?"

Joy Reid

Joy used to sub on Rachel, and the sound of her bright, snappy, slightly-bored voice was always a refreshing change from our favorite power nerd. She was sued for libel by a foaming-at-the-mouth MAGA lady named Roslyn La Liberte, who was screaming so hard about immigration at a city council meeting in California that her eyeballs look like they're exploding. Joy has also drawn the ire of Fox news on a regular basis, and many more people for busting on them for racism. Shooting-from-the-hip witch.

Natalie Wynn

This trans woman's YouTube channel is on fire. Wynn is a social critic, costume genius, entertaining drunk, and former philosophy major who can explain anything about anything. She mocks Jordan Peterson, goofs on Cancel Culture, and totally rules on the topic of Western civ.—you know, that sacred thought experiment the Left is supposed to hate.

Fiona Hill

This British-American Security Council official (former) was the White House's top Russia expert long before Trump came on the scene. She was going to work for him. Her colleagues and friends told her not to. But the fate of this truth-teller was already sewn up. She was going to testify for ten hours as Lieutenant Colonel Alexander Vindman's former boss, and see his reputation destroyed, after she had resigned from her job. A dedicated non-partisan, Fiona has a new identity as Last Witch Standing.

Judy Chicago

You've never been to a dinner party like this one. When you walk into the dedicated room at the Brooklyn Museum, the give-it-all-away beauty of her multimedia feminist artwork grabs you by the throat. Ms. Chicago had been on the scene for a long time, doing things no other woman would try, and getting tons of shit from the male art establishment. She did it her way. She won. Witch? She's like 30 of 'em.

Emma Gonzalez

She became a major spokeswoman for gun control after the Marjorie Stoneman Douglass mass shooting, and like her classmate David Hogg, she took a lot of shit for it. Wiping her tears, she excoriated her critics, who had accused the students (*the students!*) of inaction, of bullying, of ignoring the signs. Why didn't they report him?" We did. ... It was no surprise to anyone that he was the shooter. Those talking about how we shouldn't ostracize him? YOU DIDN'T KNOW THIS KID!"

Cyndi Lauper

Now, come on, Cyndi's way cooler than Madonna. Always was. A tireless, gorgeous champion of queer youth, she launched the True Colors Fund to help fight homelessness among LGBT kids; there are more than 1.6 million homeless kids out there, and 40% are LGBTQ. They get bumped, abandoned, kicked out. Bonus: she's actually a nice person. "Say it softly and learn the power of a whisper." We will, Cyndi, we will.

Michelle Obama

Fashion icon, first First Lady of color, and the person who drives Melania Trump even crazier than she already is, Michelle Obama had an unerring knack for pissing off the conservative establishment without actually doing anything offensive. It could be her air of unflappable confidence, her thousand-watt smile, or the fierce intelligence lurking behind her ebullient public persona—Michelle O. is mothering a whole new generation of women into visibility and power.

Judge Amy Berman Jackson

There aren't a lot of people who could sit up there running a trial with Trump himself breathing fire down their necks, but this woman had Roger Stone on a leash like a pug at a picnic. Her detractors tried everything. The *sang-froid* she needed for this gig was mind-blowing. Stone was his own worst enemy; his own texts and emails prove the allegations against him. Judge Jackson commented acidly that Stone's lawyers had nothing to say to the jury except "So what?" Stone didn't have to serve any of his 40 months, because Trump commuted his sentence. Guilty much?

Ieshia Evans

This young mother, a nurse, faced down riot cops in Baton Rouge after the shooting deaths of Alton Sterling and Philando Castile. Jonathan Bachman's photo became a worldwide sensation, showing the police recoiling from Evans's apparent tenderness while trying to capture her. Her six-year-old son, upon learning that Mommy had been arrested, asked, "Why? I thought only bad people got arrested." It's not always the case, his mother said.

AOC

"I was born in a place where your ZIP code determines your destiny," she says. Is Alexandria Ocasio-Cortez the quintessential millennial politician, or just the one we've been waiting for all this time? She seems to be able to slip a couple of extra hours into every day in which to find weaknesses in her opponents' ideas. It seems like every one of her risks pays off. And she's only 29.

Erica Jong

The original amped-up feminist fiction writer did more to energize young women than all the sages of the movement ever could, and that's because *Fear of Flying* was such a hoot. And beautifully-written, too—how many of its original fans remember that?—while remaining faithful to the realities of sex. Not to mention style: in a post-coital reverie, the heroine's lover, Adrian, nuzzles her sex and pronounces it slimy. "Your slime," the heroine, Isadora, says.

"'Our slime,' he corrected me."

In such precise moments, movements are born.

Maxine Waters

Looking down at you over her reading glasses with that weary disapproval in her voice, the tigress of California's 43rd district would be your worst nightmare if you ever tried to put one over on her, or happen to be Steve Mnuchin. Why wasn't he responding to the letters she was sending him? To which his answer was, "Thank you for your service to the State of California!" "Reclaiming my time," she barked while he tried to squirm out from under her paralyzing stare. She should have branded that phrase on his ass: dollars to doughnuts he still feels it.

Dolly Parton

The "I'm not dumb, and I'm sure not blonde" superstar saved lives this past year with her donation to COVID research that helped result in a vaccine. Yes, she's that smart and that cool, saying "Do we think our little white asses are the only ones that matter?" Once we get rid of the Nathan Bedford Forrest statue in Nashville, let's have one of Dolly. And yes, she can play the F out of that banjo.

Elizabeth Warren

Elizabeth Warren is actually a real person, and not a very big one. She's kind of petite, like a middle-school teacher. And her constant determination to explain herself puts her in a different category than any other political figure, except maybe Bernie. She leads with utter sincerity, and a bit of frustration too. Wonky superpowers might not get you everywhere, but the White House would have worked just fine.

AVE FEMINAM

Marie Yovanovich

Marie "Masha" Yovanovich, former U.S. ambassador to Ukraine, got canned by Donald Trump after a career of distinguished work for the Foreign Service because of a perceived lack of, shall we say, desire to get with the program. Rudy abhorred her anti-corruption stance; Trump ranted, "Get rid of her!...Take her out. Okay? Do it." Yovanovich had no axe to grind at the first impeachment hearings—but if she was scared, and she should have been, you couldn't see it. Ice-cold witch here. We need more of her.

Chrissie Hynde

Our favorite vegetarian, animal-rights witch, Chrissie Hynde sings in a dark contralto that seems like it spent some time buried in a cellar along with some magic beans and a copy of *Answered Prayers*. That tremor in her voice, her sarcasm—"when you own a big piece of the bloody third world, the babies just come with the scenery"—brings the message that every inch won from the miseries of life is cause for celebration, or at least one more beer.

Hillary Clinton

An astronaut who wasn't allowed to leave the ground, Clinton will have to watch the arcs of women who followed her. A post-political life will be an earthbound place for this explorer. She has earned her place among the stars.

Bette Midler

Her 1972 album, "The Divine Miss M," brought her straight from the Continental Baths in the basement of New York's Ansonia Hotel to the turntables of America. Faithful to her first audience—gay men—she can do kitsch like nobody else, but a serious song like John Prine's "Hello In There" shows her at the apex of her powers: unzipping your heart with her voice, and climbing in.

Darnella Frazier

One afternoon's circumstances forced this high school senior to become the shepherd of a movement. But all Darnella Frazier thought she was doing was taking her little cousin for a snack. She's the one who videoed the murder of George Floyd, and afterward had to fight off accusations of greed and arrogance. She poured out her courage, no matter what it cost her. We can't give her wings, but we hope she'll accept this broom. Fly high, Darnella.

Christine Blasey Ford

Few rewards, and plenty of dangers, awaited this witch as she testified against the nomination of party boy Brett Kavanaugh to the Supreme Court. She told the Senate Judiciary Committee how Kavanaugh held her down in a bedroom with his hand over her mouth when she was a teen. Dr. Ford admitted later that the backlash was worse than she'd expected. But given the necessity of living the truth, she'd do it again. Dr. Ford galvanized the nation and showed how a dauntless woman behaves.

Cardi B

Now that we're all talking about what she gets away with, and whether she *should* get away with it, we might as well admit that Cardi B is as clever as hell, and also really funny. Along with Megan Thee Stallion in WAP, sneaking down a Dr. Caligari hallway like someone's horny idea of Betty Boop, she turns her quest for satisfaction into a kind of litmus test for how much her audience really wants to know about what girls like. She can call your bluff and make you love her for it.

Ana Kasparian

The icy calm of this Young Turk broadcaster should scare people. Ana Kasparian can, if she wants to, demonstrate to the world that everything you do is wrong. *TYT* (The Young Turks), a show she shares with Cenk Uygur, is totally unscripted, and usually features Ana doing what she does so well: making some powerful person look like an asshole. By the way, "Young Turks" is a phrase that means "rebels." Cenk is indeed Turkish-American, but Ana's family is Armenian.

Amanda Gorman

At Joseph R. Biden Jr.'s inauguration, Amanda Gorman stepped up to the podium with a sky-high hairdo and bewitching foxy eyes to read "The Hill We Climb," and the parents of America wondered if it wouldn't be a good thing if their kids grew up to be poets. "The new dawn balloons as we free it," she intoned, and the traditional weather/landscape/light in American poetry spilled out into the ears of worried people from the mouth of a twenty-two-year-old Black woman. Things might be all right after all.

Deb Haaland

As the first indigenous cabinet secretary in U.S. history, Deb Haaland was sworn in to her post as Secretary of the Interior in a traditional ribbon skirt appliquéed with a cornstalk, a symbol of her tribe. Haaland, a member of the Pueblo of Laguna, immediately proposed strict limitations of oil and gas drilling on public lands, infuriating the fossil fuel industry.

Marcia Fudge

The 18th Secretary of the U.S. Department of Housing and Urban Development walked up to the podium in the White House press room, said "Good afternoon," and, getting no response, tugged her earlobe as if the sound to her head had been turned off.

"Good afternoon," she began again, and this time got a chorus of greetings.

"This is your Black auntie," the Twitterverse chortled. "The congregation gonna learn today."

Letitia James

Tish James is the Attorney General of New York, the first African-American and the first woman to be elected to the position. She knocked Governor Cuomo off his pedestal by releasing a scathing report on nursing homes' lack of compliance and their undercounting of COVID deaths. On top of that, she's all over the Trump organization like white on rice for possible cheating on loans and tax benefits. She's suing the NRA, taking on Google and Facebook...She's got so many reins of dangerous power in her hands, she could be racing a chariot in the Roman coliseum. Bet on her.

Fani Willis

Fani Willis is the Fulton County DA. That means she's in the center of Georgia—Atlanta and suburbs surrounding it—and *that* means she's holding the hottest hot potato right now. Opening a criminal investigation into the Former Guy's call to Brad Raffensberger to "find" him some votes put Atlanta in the national spotlight, and the GOP is trying to water down its influence by bringing in the rest of the (whiter, more conservative) state to serve on a grand jury.

Nicolle Wallace

One of the fab trio of commentators (along with Rachel and Joy) who's chewed on Trump all last year, Nicolle was the White House Communications Director under Dubya, and worked for John McCain. Trump dubbed her a "third-rate lapdog" last year, which means (definitely!) she's doing something right. "Thrown off *The View* like a dog," the former guy said after Wallace opined that the right was trying to smear Biden. Bow wow.

Park Cannon

Park Cannon is the woman who went to knock on Brian Kemp's door when he and a bunch of other white dinosaurs locked themselves in to sign anti-voting legislation in Georgia. They had her dragged away in handcuffs and booked on a felony charge. They had to let her go, of course, but they kept her overnight in a jail cell, just in case she was thinking there was anything wrong with what *they* were doing. Fun fact: Kemp has a painting of a plantation over his desk, which goes nicely with the legislation they were signing. It's a really bad painting.

SALLY ECKHOFF BIO:

A former critic for the *New York Times* and the *Village Voice*, Sally Eckhoff is also a visual artist, animator, and rider. Sally's short, hand-drawn animations have appeared in film festivals around the US and Europe; she's currently working on the pilot of *Beastly Lives*, a podcast on animals, art, and adventure. She lives in the Hudson Valley of New York State with her black cat, Sharpie, and continues to ride and train Spot, her pinto horse.

Sally is also the author of the memoirs *F*ck Art (Let's Dance)* and *How Horses Get Their Names*, and the author and illustrator of *F*ck Art: A Downtown Coloring Book*. This is her second coloring book.

OTHER BOOKS
by SALLY ECKHOFF

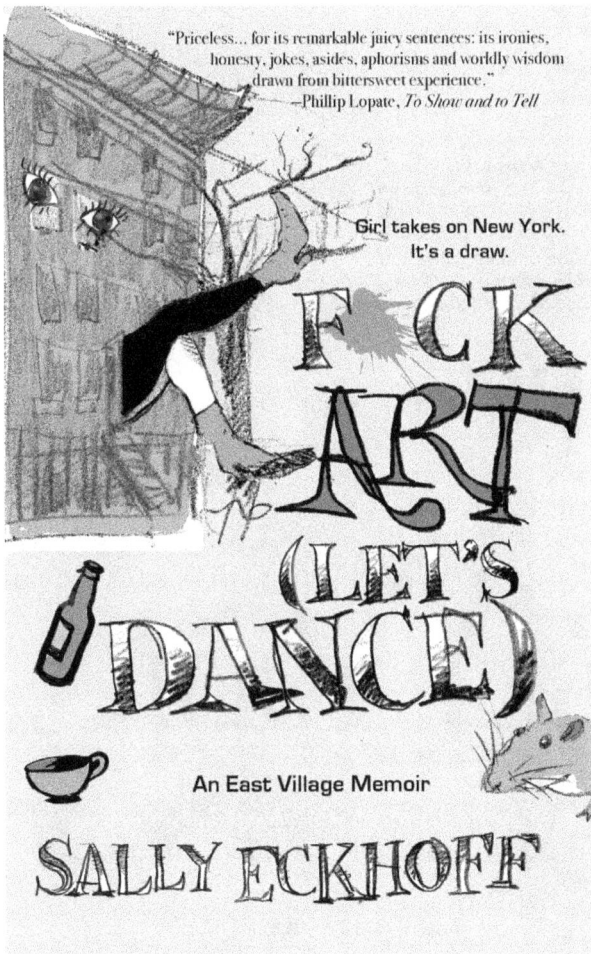

"Priceless... for its remarkable juicy sentences: its ironies, honesty, jokes, asides, aphorisms and worldly wisdom drawn from bittersweet experience."
—Phillip Lopate, *To Show and to Tell*

Girl takes on New York.
It's a draw.

F*CK ART (LET'S DANCE)

An East Village Memoir

SALLY ECKHOFF

F*ck Art (Let's Dance)

*F*ck Art (Let's Dance)* is a chronicle of ten slam-bang years in a very slam-bang part of New York City, and of one young painter's crusade to make that place her own.

This memoir, by a former *Village Voice* writer and critic, starts in 1977 with the Summer of Sam and ends with the Tompkins Square Park riots—two notorious incidents that defined an age. After a last, desperate summer in the beach towns of Long Island, the naive young wannabe artist borrows her dad's El Camino, finances a trip to Manhattan with the change on his cufflink stand, and rents an apartment on East Tenth Street with a floor so crooked that everything that falls off the kitchen counter rolls under the bathtub. And then she begins to paint, eat, dance, and *feel* her way around New York.

*F*ck Art* might remind you of what it feels like to be a beginner in a land of crooks and geniuses.

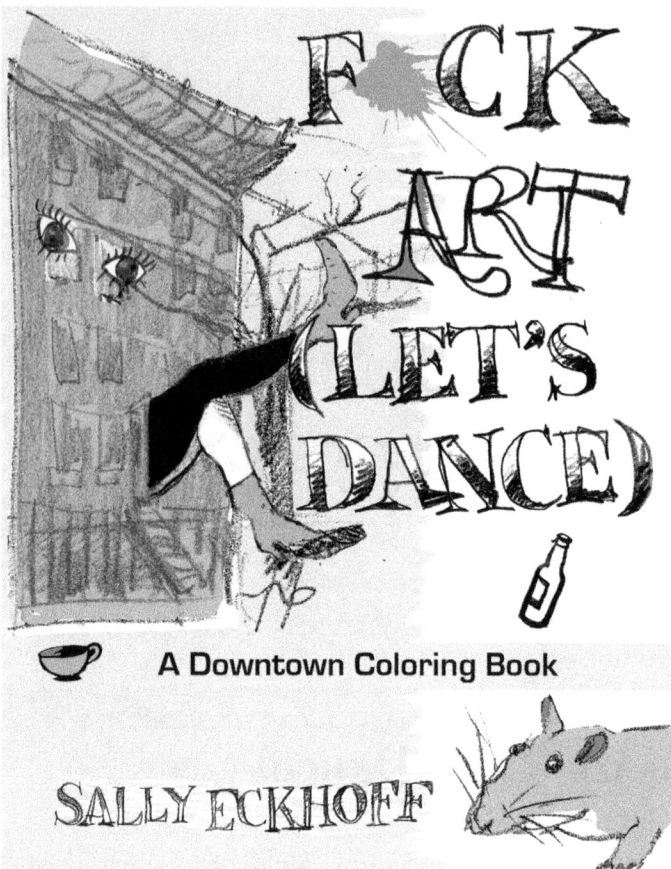

F*ck Art: A Downtown Coloring Book

In *F*ck Art (Let's Dance)*, author and artist Sally Eckhoff told the story of the downtown art and music scene in New York in the last decade during which a starving artist could afford to eat (and sing and paint and dance) in Manhattan. In *F*ck Art: A Downtown Coloring Book*, she recreates that scene as a punk art coloring book for adults.

How Horses Get Their Names

A pat of courage. Doesn't everybody need one? Picture yourself moving to the country. There are going to be a few things you haven't accounted for. Nature, time, and weather have way more leverage when it comes to throwing your plans out of whack. And when you wander off the path so far you don't even know you're lost, you're going to need a friend. People are OK. But you'd probably be better off with a horse.

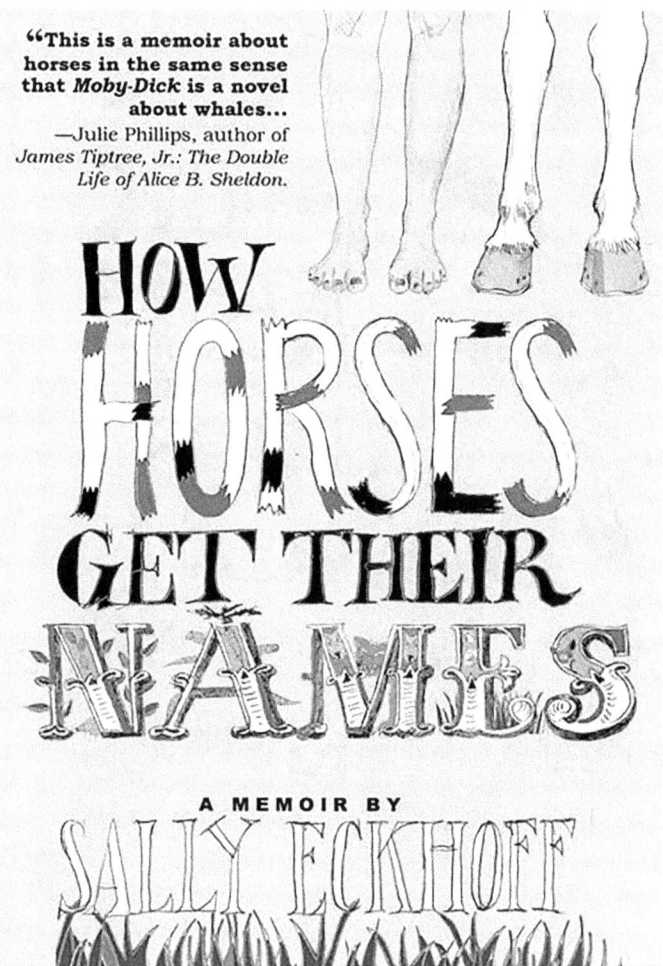

"This is a memoir about horses in the same sense that *Moby-Dick* is a novel about whales...
—Julie Phillips, author of *James Tiptree, Jr.: The Double Life of Alice B. Sheldon.*

www.ingramcontent.com/pod-product-compliance
Lightning Source LLC
Chambersburg PA
CBHW081332090426

42737CB00017B/3109